W9-BXE-205

LIVING WELL

LIVING WITH ASTHMA

by Shirley Wimbish Gray

THE CHILD'S WORLD®
CHANHASSEN, MINNESOTA

The Child's World®

The publisher wishes to sincerely thank Sharon Ficarrotta, C.P.N.P., for her help in preparing this book for publication.

Published in the United States of America by The Child's World®
P.O. Box 326
Chanhassen, MN 55317-0326
800-599-READ
www.childsworld.com

Photo Credits: Cover: RubberBall Productions/Corbis, Custom Medical Stock Photo, Inc. (inset); Lynne Sladky/Associated Press: 5; Corbis: 20 (top), 25; Lester V. Bergman/ Corbis: 8 (bottom); Bettmann/Corbis: 20 (bottom), 21; Angela Hampton/Corbis: 9; RubberBall Productions/Corbis: 1; EyeWire/GettyImages: 26, 29; The Image Bank/ GettyImages: 6, 7, 27; PhotoDisc/GettyImages: 15, 23; Stone/GettyImages: 17, 18, 24; Custom Medical Stock Photo, Inc.: 8 (top), 13; Bonnie Kamin/PhotoEdit: 22; Michael Newman/PhotoEdit: 16; Tom Prettyman/PhotoEdit: 12; Robin L. Sachs/ PhotoEdit: 14; Mark E. Gibson/Unicorn Stock Photos:10; Herbert L. Stormont/ Unicorn Stock Photos: 19

The Child's World®: Mary Berendes, Publishing Director

Editorial Directions, Inc.: E. Russell Primm, Editor; Alice Flanagan, Photo Researcher; Linda S. Koutris, Photo Selector; The Design Lab, Designer and Page Production; Red Line Editorial, Fact Researcher; Irene Keller, Copy Editor; Tim Griffin/IndexServ, Indexer; Donna Frassetto, Proofreader

Library of Congress Cataloging-in-Publication Data
Gray, Shirley W.
  Living with asthma / by Shirley Wimbish Gray.
    v. cm. — (Living Well series)
Includes index.
Contents: Do you know someone who has asthma?—What is asthma?—What's it like to have asthma?—Who gets asthma?—What can we do about asthma?—Will we ever cure asthma?
  ISBN 1-56766-100-9
  1. Asthma—Juvenile literature. 2. Asthma in children—Juvenile literature. [1. Asthma. 2. Diseases.] I. Title. II. Series.
  RC591 .G73 2002
  618.92'238—dc21
                                                    2002002866

TABLE OF CONTENTS

CHAPTER ONE

Do You Know Someone Who Has Asthma?

When Amy Van Dyken was six years old, her doctor said she

should start swimming. He thought it would help her asthma. Amy's

asthma was bad. She was 12 years old before she could swim all the

way across the pool.

Amy, her family, and her doctor worked to control the asthma.

Her coaches and her teammates helped with her swimming. Her

asthma got better—and so did her swimming.

In 1996, Amy became the first American woman to win four

gold medals at one Olympic Games. In 2000, she won another gold

medal in swimming at the Sydney Olympics.

Maybe you know somebody who has asthma. Or maybe you

have asthma yourself. One out of every 14 children has asthma. It is

Amy Van Dyken holds one of her four Olympic gold medals.

the most common **chronic** disease in children. Learning more

about asthma is one way to help those who have it. Then they can

reach their goals like Amy did.

CHAPTER TWO

WHAT IS ASTHMA?

Asthma is a disease of the immune system. This system protects your body against germs. A virus is a germ that causes lots of different infections. One of these is a head cold. When you have a cold, the **white blood cells** in your body get busy. They cause other cells to make a chemical called histamine (HISS-tuh-meen). The histamine makes your nose run. Your runny nose is a sign that your immune system is getting rid of the virus!

People with asthma have immune systems that react to ordinary things in

The runny nose you get with a head cold shows that your immune system is fighting off a virus.

The pollen on this tree can cause an asthma attack.

the air. Our bodies take in tiny pieces of dust when we breathe. The dust could be **pollen** from flowers. It could also be **dander** from a cat. When people have asthma, their immune system attacks the dust just like it attacks germs. Lots of histamine is made. This can cause an asthma attack, or flare-up.

An asthma attack affects the **respiratory system.** This system helps your body breathe in oxygen. It also helps you

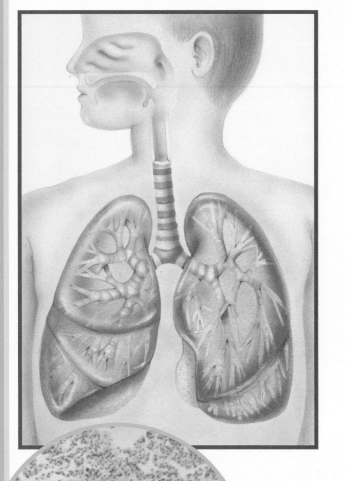

breathe out carbon dioxide—
the gas in your blood that is
released into the lungs and
breathed out. Your nose and
mouth are part of your
respiratory system. So is your
windpipe, your lungs, and
your air tubes, or airways.

The muscles that wrap around the
air tubes are loose. They move easily
during breathing. The lining inside
the air tubes is thin, so lots of air moves
through the tubes. The air goes to the
air sacs in the lungs.

*This illustration (above) shows the
respiratory system of a child. Below is
a magnified view of the air tubes in
a person with asthma.*

During an asthma attack, however, the cells in the lungs make too much histamine. The histamine tightens the muscles around the air tubes. This sudden tightening is called a spasm. The lining inside the tubes swells. The tubes may fill with fluid, or mucus. Very little air moves through the tubes

The medicine inside an inhaler helps people breathe easier during an asthma attack.

when this happens, so breathing becomes very hard.

The good news is that people with asthma can learn to prevent most attacks. And, if an attack starts, they can take medicine. Then they can breathe easier.

CHAPTER THREE

WHAT'S IT LIKE TO
HAVE ASTHMA?

Children with asthma can run and jump. They can play baseball

and soccer. They can be cheerleaders or sing in a choir. They can do

most of the things their friends do. But they also have to learn what

to do if their asthma flares up.

Soccer is just one of the many sports people who have asthma can enjoy.

Asthma attacks are not all alike. Sometimes the attacks make people cough. Sometimes people feel like they cannot catch their breath. Some people make a noise like a whistle when they breathe in. That noise is called "wheezing."

Medicine makes it easier to breathe during an attack. Most of these medicines are **inhaled,** or breathed in through the mouth or nose. They work in just a few minutes. Some relax the muscles in the airway. Other types of medicine reduce the swelling in the airway.

Many people with asthma carry an **inhaler** with them all the time. The inhaler is filled with medicine to help stop the attack. Children with asthma may keep extra inhalers at school. Then if they have an attack, they can get the medicine fast.

Adults and children should test their lungs every day. They can use a tool called a peak-flow meter. It looks a little like a kazoo. It

The medicine inside the inhaler this boy is using reduces the swelling in his airways.

helps them to know whether an asthma attack might start.

To use the peak-flow meter, you must blow hard into one end. The air pushes a little bar along the top. People with asthma know how far they should be able to push the bar. If the bar does not move enough, they know that their asthma might flare up soon. Then they can take extra medicine to prevent it.

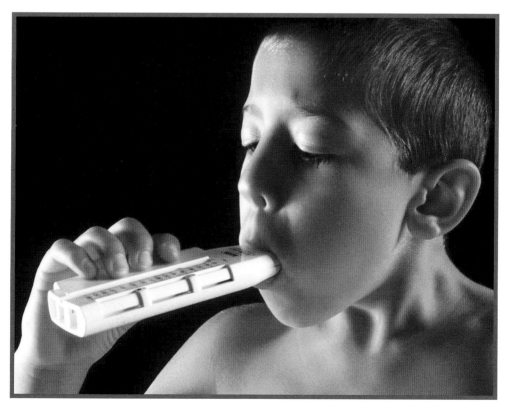

This boy is using a peak-flow meter.

Most asthma attacks are easy to stop. Others can be scary, though. Sometimes, during an attack, people get too tired to walk. They breathe fast. Their chest may sink in when they try to breathe. Their fingernails may turn blue. These are signs that they are not getting enough oxygen. They need to go to the hospital right away.

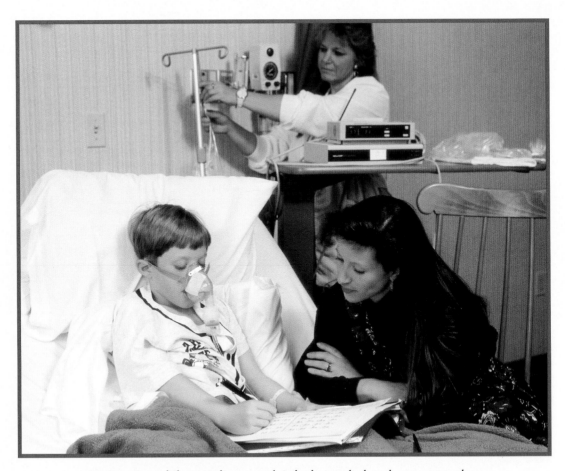

Once in awhile an asthma attack is bad enough that the person needs to go to a hospital for treatment.

A doctor or nurse gives oxygen to someone who is having trouble breathing. Extra medicine might also help. Soon the person should start breathing easily again. Sometimes people die because they do not get medical help quickly enough during a bad asthma attack.

An asthma flare-up may last a couple of hours

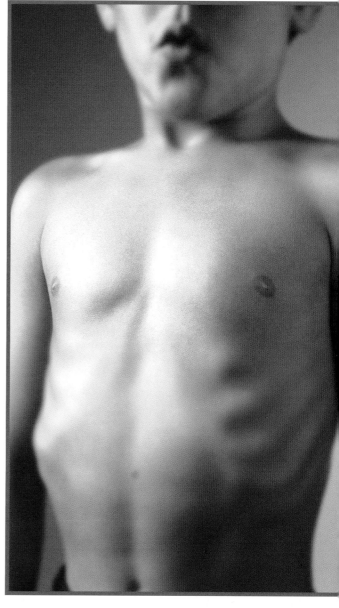

During a bad asthma attack the person's chest may sink in like this boy's.

or longer. When it is over, breathing returns to normal. It might be days, weeks, or even months before another flare-up occurs.

CHAPTER FOUR

WHAT CAN WE DO
ABOUT ASTHMA?

Doctors don't know what causes asthma to flare up. But they know that some things can **trigger** an asthma attack. Pollen and animal dander are common triggers. So are dust mites and smoke. Some children have asthma attacks when they catch a cold or have a sore throat. Others have asthma attacks when they laugh or cry.

People with asthma learn to stay away from their triggers. A child with asthma might not be able to have a cat as a pet. The dander on the cat could be a trigger. A fish would make a better pet.

Fish are great pets in homes where asthma is a problem.

16

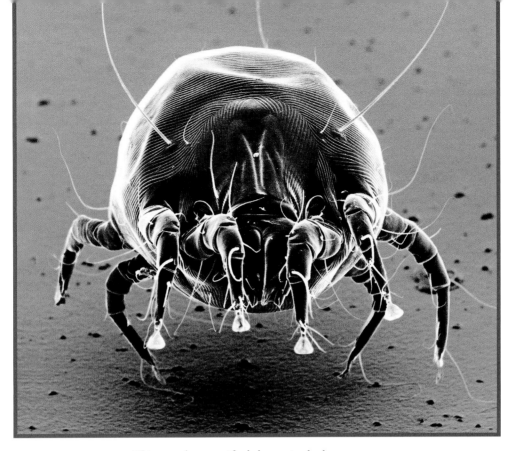

This greatly magnified dust mite looks very scary.
Dust mites can increase the possibility of asthma attacks.

Staying away from dust is hard. Washing bedspreads and pillows every week in hot water is one way to get rid of dust mites. Some people with asthma decide not to have carpets on their floors. This also helps to control dust.

Cigarette smoke is a common trigger. Children who live with adults who smoke often have asthma. These children may have lots

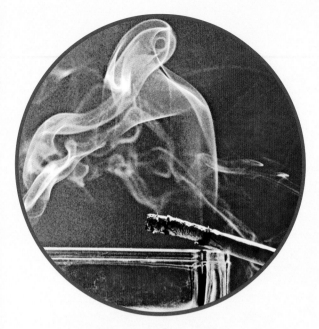

Cigarette smoke is another cause of asthma attacks.

of trouble breathing unless the adult quits smoking. Some children have such bad attacks caused by cigarette smoke that they have to go to the hospital.

Running and playing hard can trigger an asthma attack in some children and adults. This is called exercise-induced (EK-sur-size in-DYOOSD) asthma. Some professional athletes have this form. They have to be careful. They could have an asthma attack in the middle of a football game or a race. They have to stop and use their inhalers. Then they should breathe easily again.

Using medicine is a good way to keep a flare-up from starting.

These medicines are inhaled or taken by mouth. Your friends with asthma may take these types of drugs every morning and every night. They do this even when they spend the night at someone else's house.

Antihistamine also helps people with asthma. It keeps the body from making too much histamine. This is good for someone whose trigger is

Athletes with asthma should always have an inhaler close at hand in case they have an attack while playing their sport.

pollen. Trees give off lots of pollen in the spring when they grow new leaves. Many people take antihistamine pills in spring.

CHAPTER FIVE

WHO GETS ASTHMA?

Do you know what Teddy Roosevelt and John F. Kennedy had in common? They both became president of the United States, and they both had asthma. Lots of other famous people have asthma, too. Basketball stars Dennis Rodman and Dominique Wilkins have it. Olympic swimmer Debbie Meyer and diver Greg Louganis also have asthma.

U.S. president John F. Kennedy (above) had asthma as does Olympian Debbie Meyer (below).

No one knows why one person develops asthma and another does not. Everyone's immune system reacts to pollen and other dust in the air, but only some of us have asthma. A child with asthma might have a parent who had it. But sometimes no one else in the family has asthma.

Asthma starts at any age, but it is most common

Many people call Jackie Joyner-Kersee the greatest female athlete ever. She competed in track and field. That meant she had to run faster and jump farther than everyone else.

When Jackie was in college, she started having trouble breathing. She thought she was not in good shape and needed to work out harder. Then the doctor told her she had asthma. At first she did not do what the doctor told her to do. Then she had even more trouble breathing. Finally, she started to learn about asthma and to use her inhaler.

After that, Jackie won a total of six medals at four different Olympic Games. She is glad she finally learned how to control her asthma.

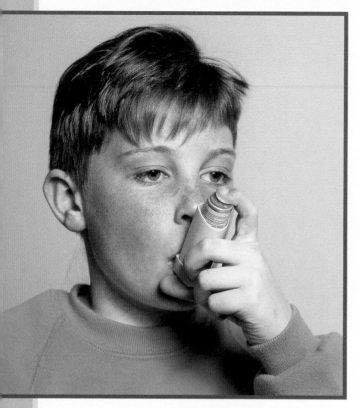

No one knows why asthma is a growing problem among children in the United States.

in school-age children. The number of children and adults with asthma is growing every year. More than twice as many people have asthma today as had it in 1980. The number of people who have died from asthma has also increased. No one knows the reason for all this.

Some people think air pollution (puh-LOO-shuhn) may be to blame. The air around most cities is cleaner now than it was in 1980, though. So scientists do not think air pollution is the reason. They wonder if the air inside buildings is a problem, however. Maybe people spend more time indoors now than people did in the past.

*Some scientists think that asthma may be increasing because
we spend more time inside, such as in this office.*

Triggers like dust mites and cockroaches can be a problem indoors,

and so can tobacco smoke.

Look around at the children in your class. Do any of your

classmates have asthma? Chances are at least one or two of them do.

Maybe even your teacher does!

CHAPTER SIX

WILL WE EVER CURE ASTHMA?

In India, people used to treat asthma by practicing yoga. Today, millions of people in the United States and around the world enjoy yoga.

The word *asthma* comes from a Greek word meaning "to pant or breathe hard." Over the years, people have tried many things to help cure the hard breathing of asthma.

In the 1100s, a doctor in Egypt suggested chicken soup to a prince who had asthma. In India, doctors taught their patients to do yoga. Early Native American tribes were the first to try smoking tobacco. Smoking tobacco became a popular asthma remedy in Europe.

In the 1800s, doctors told people with asthma to smoke cigarettes and pipes. They used the smoke to help get medicine to the lungs. Later, people spent time at health spas. They hoped clean water, clean air, and sunlight would help their asthma.

In many areas of the world, people treated asthma by smoking cigarettes and pipes. We now know that tobacco smoke can cause asthma.

Doctors know more about asthma today than doctors did hundreds of years ago. Even so, they still have lots of questions. Why do more people have asthma now than had asthma twenty years ago? Why are more children in inner cities developing asthma? How can someone stop an asthma attack once it starts? Can there ever be a cure for asthma?

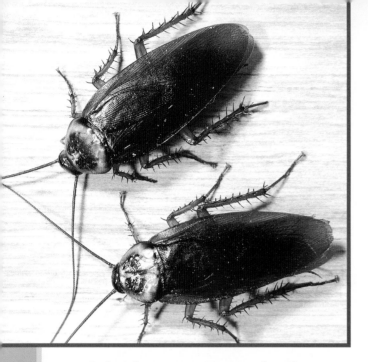

Cockroaches are common triggers for asthma.

Scientists are looking for clues so that they can answer these questions. For example, scientists know that cockroaches are common triggers for asthma. Cockroaches like to live in dark, moist places. They are often found under houses and in damp, old wood. Children who live in old or poor neighborhoods often develop asthma. Could they be reacting to the insects in their houses?

Scientists and doctors need help to answer these questions. Sometimes they ask people with asthma to take part in **clinical trials.** These are studies that test new ideas for treating asthma. Children can be a part of clinical trials. When they do, they become part of the research team.

You can help, too. Do you know someone who has asthma? If so, be a good friend. Learn what triggers your friend's asthma. Then find ways to avoid those triggers. You might help a friend remember to take an inhaler on a school field trip. Controlling asthma is hard work. Having a friend helps.

Dust mites are a common trigger for people with asthma. What exactly is a dust mite and why is it such a problem? Dust mites are tiny bugs. They belong to the same family as spiders and ticks. They are so tiny that you need a microscope to see them. Mites live where they can find their favorite food. They eat the dead skin that falls off people and pets. Pillows and beds are great homes for mites. So are stuffed chairs and rugs.

As dust mites grow, they shed their skin. Their dead skin and body wastes become triggers for people with asthma.

Glossary

chronic (KRON-ik) If something is chronic, it is something a person lives with every day.

clinical trials (KLIN-ik-uhl TRYE-uhls) Clinical trials are studies that test new ideas for treating an illness.

dander (DAN-duhr) Dander is tiny flakes of dead skin from dogs, cats, and other animals.

inhaled (in-HAYLD) Something inhaled is breathed in.

inhaler (in-HAY-luhr) An inhaler is a small container that sends a puff of medicine through the mouth to the lungs.

pollen (POL-uhn) Pollen is the tiny yellow grains produced by flowers.

respiratory system (RESS-pi-ruh-taw-ree SISS-tuhm) The respiratory system is the body's system of air-breathing organs including the lungs.

trigger (TRIG-uhr) To trigger something is to cause it or to set it in motion.

white blood cells (WITE BLUHD SELS) White blood cells are tiny cells in the bloodstream that normally fight disease.

Questions and Answers about Asthma

What is asthma? Asthma is a disease of the immune system. When the immune system overreacts to ordinary things such as pollen and dust, it causes an asthma attack, or flare-up.

How many people have asthma? In 1998, almost 17 million Americans had asthma. Of that number, almost 4.8 million were children.

Who gets asthma? Anyone can develop asthma at any age. Sometimes a child with asthma has a parent who had asthma as a child. Often people with allergies also have asthma.

How is asthma treated? It is best to avoid things that trigger an asthma flare-up, such as cat dander and tobacco smoke. Using medicine daily can help prevent an attack. After an attack begins, inhaled medicine can help stop it.

Will a person who has asthma ever get rid of it? Some children will outgrow asthma. Others will have it even as adults. Sometimes people do not develop asthma until they are more than 60 or 70 years old.

Can I catch asthma from someone else? No. Even if you are near a friend who coughs during an asthma attack, you cannot catch it.

How can you treat asthma? The best way to prevent asthma attacks is by staying away from things that trigger them. It is important to use medicine if your doctor says so.

Helping a Friend Who Has Asthma

▷ Learn what your friend's triggers are. Then plan activities that avoid the triggers.

▷ Get your friend's inhaler if an attack begins.

▷ Go find an adult while your friend uses the inhaler.

▷ Call 911 if your friend's breathing gets worse.

▷ Never tease or make fun of your friend because of the asthma.

Did You Know?

▷ Stuffed animal toys can collect dust and trigger an asthma attack.

▷ In 1995, asthma caused more than 1.8 million emergency-room visits.

▷ Officials in New York City told people to wear masks over their nose and mouth after the destruction of the World Trade Center Towers on September 11, 2001. The masks helped protect them from the thick smoke and dust that could have triggered asthma attacks.

▷ More than 5,000 people die of asthma each year in the United States.

How to Learn
More about Asthma

At the Library: Nonfiction
Carter, Alden R., and Siri Carter.
I'm Tougher than Asthma.
Morton Grove, Ill.: Albert Whitman & Company, 1999.

Flanagan, Alice K.
Mrs. Murphy Fights Fires.
Danbury, Conn.: Children's Press, 1998.

Gosselin, Kim.
Sportsercise!: A School Story about Exercise-Induced Asthma.
Valley Park, Mo.: JayJo Books, 1997.

Weiss, J. H.
Breathe Easy.
Washington, D.C.: Magination Press, 1994

At the Library: Fiction
Gosselin, Kim.
Taking Asthma to Camp: A Fictional Story about Asthma Camp.
Valley Park, Mo.: JayJo Books, 1998.

London, Jonathan, and Nadine Bernard Westcott (Illustrator).
The Lion Who Had Asthma.
Morton Grove, Ill.: Albert Whitman & Company, 1997.

On the Web
Visit our home page for lots of links about asthma:
http://www.childsworld.com/links.html

Note to Parents, Teachers, and Librarians: We routinely verify our
Web links to make sure they're safe, active sites—so encourage your
readers to check them out!

Through the Mail or by Phone

Allergy and Asthma Network/Mothers of Asthmatics, Inc.
2751 Prosperity Avenue, Suite 150
Fairfax, VA 22031
800/878-4403 or 703/641-9595

American Academy of Allergy, Asthma, and Immunology
611 East Wells Street
Milwaukee, WI 53202
414/272-6071

The American Lung Association
1740 Broadway
New York, NY 10019
212/315-8700

Asthma and Allergy Foundation of America
1233 20th Street, N.W.
Suite 402
Washington, DC 20036
202/466-7643 or 800/7-ASTHMA

The University of Chicago Asthma Center
5841 S. Maryland Avenue
MC 6076
Chicago, IL 60637
773/702-0880

On Video

Managing Asthma at School: Making a Difference
This video is free by writing to:
NHLBI Information Center
P.O. Box 30105
Bethesda, MD 20824-0105

Index

About the Author

Shirley Wimbish Gray has been a writer and educator for more than 25 years and has published more than a dozen nonfiction books for children. She also coordinates cancer education programs at the University of Arkansas for Medical Sciences and consults as a writer with scientists and physicians. She lives with her husband and two sons in Little Rock, Arkansas.